LADYBIRD AND FRIENDS

Nester Kadzviti Murira

Once upon a time insects in the valley below the mountain

slope met every morning for a chat. One morning the friends,

met by the tall grass near a small pond.

"Good morning Ladybird. That's a very smart coat you are

wearing", said the Wasp.

Isn't it nice to meet you, I can have an excuse for stopping to rest." The Dung Beetle said from behind a huge ball of animal waste she was pushing with her strong spiky hind legs.

"Your coat is indeed lovely, Ladybird. I like the round black spots on the red". The Beetle said looking at the ladybird's red and black coat.

"Oh thank you, Beetle." Mrs. Ladybird said smiling proudly.

"I cannot take my eyes off your smart coat, Mrs.Ladybird. How do you keep your coat so clean?" Mrs. Spider asked her eyes still on Mrs. Ladybird's coat.

"I wash in the early morning dew." Mrs. Ladybird said proudly. "I then sit on shiny clean leaves while having my breakfast of the fattest aphids. The morning sun's rays shine on my coat and make it bright and beautiful". Mrs. Ladybird explained smiling to her friends.

I have always admired you Miss Wasp especially your beautiful slim waist. I think that is a great shape."

"Do you really mean it?" Miss Wasp asked smiling and looking down her body proudly.

"Well, my shape helps me a lot to bend my body when building my nest, picking food and of course when I want to fight my enemies with a good sting."

"Well," said Mr. Dragonfly, "with such bright colours Mrs. Ladybird, the birds cannot miss you. Very soon, the stalk will get you!"

"The stalk can come for any one of us! Who is safe with these birds flying above us? They see us before we do. We are lucky we have these leaves around us. We can hide under them until the bird flies away." Miss Beetle said.

"I cannot sit still for one moment. I have to keep flying from

one blade of grass to the other around ponds to keep safe."

Mr. Dragonfly said.

"You all know that my enemies come to have a drink of water at the pond where I live. I have to be alert all the time."

"I can kick hard with my strong hind legs and scratch too with the spikes on my legs." Mrs. Grasshopper said.

"If a bird should ever come for me, I will give him a really nasty sting he can never forget," said Mr. Busy Bee buzzing from one flower to the other.

Mrs. Ladybird, Mr. Beetle, Mrs. Grasshopper, Miss Wasp, Miss Spider and Mr. Dragonfly laughed loudly. "Ha, ha, ha! Ho, ho, ho! Gee, gee, gee! Zee, zee, zee! Do you think when a bird comes for you there will be time to think of a sting?"

They all laughed heartily.

"I can always try." Mr. Busy Bee said.

Mrs.Ladybird raised her head and said,

"There is no safe place for me. It is not always safe under the leaves. There are chameleons and frogs waiting under there all the time. One just has to be careful always."

"Always look around where you are or before you stop to pick food or take a rest." Miss Spider said.

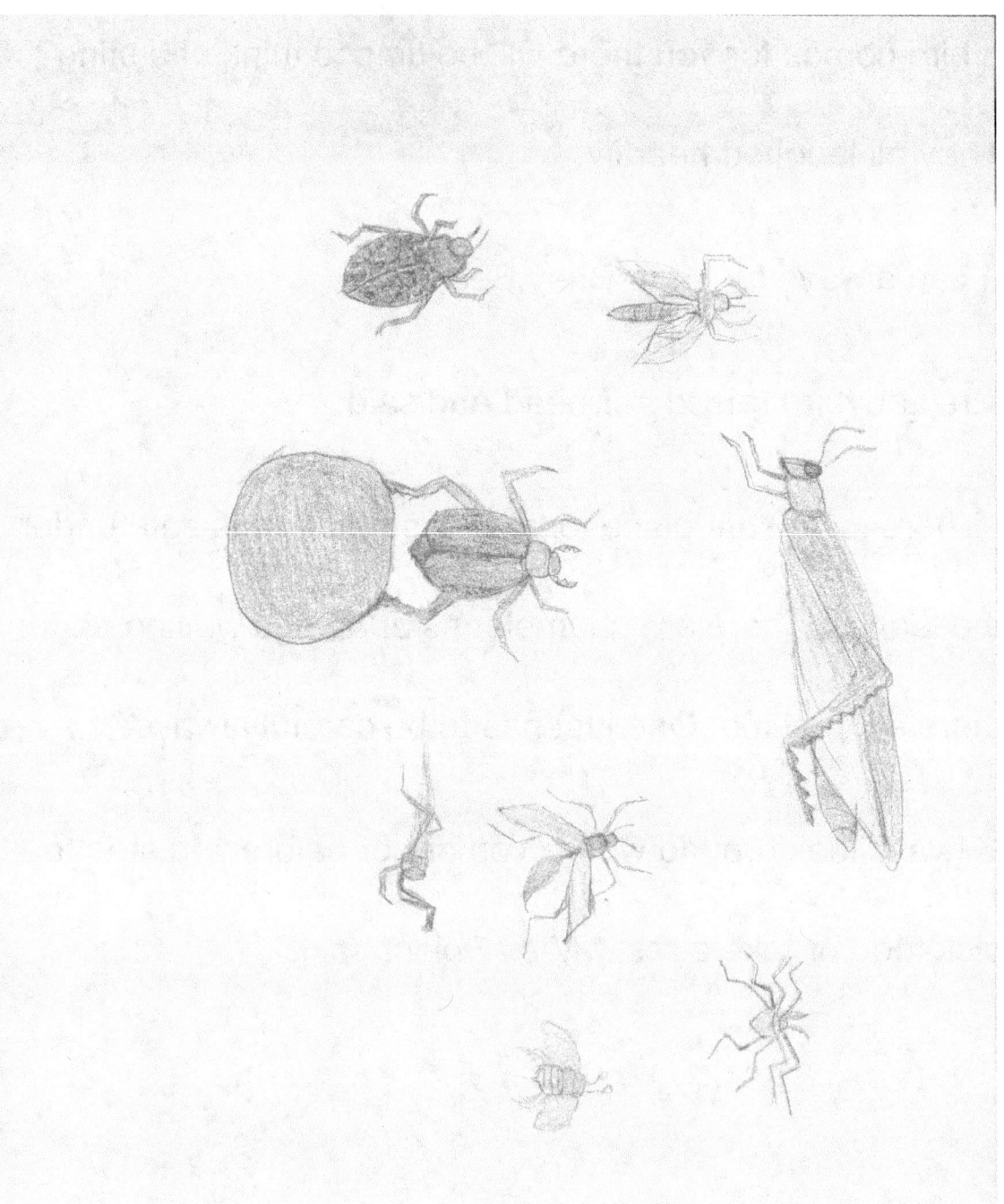

"That is true" agreed Mr. Beetle.

"Don't you ever get tired of making your endless journeys to fetch nectar and water, dear Mr. Busy Bee?" Miss Wasp asked smiling at Mr. Busy Bee.

"My little brothers and sisters in the beehive need food. My uncles, big brothers and I have to visit the parks and go across the forests to fetch water and look for nectar at least twice a day."

You come from a very big family, Mr. Bee. That is why you are always so busy." Mr. Dragonfly said looking at Mr. Busy Bee collecting nectar from the flowers.

"Oh, yes, indeed, there are many of us in my family. My mother, the Queen Bee, looks after each one of us well." Mr. Busy Bee said.

"We never go hungry. We keep busy gathering food for everyone in the family".

"Well, aren't we all busy?" Miss Spider said looking up at her new web.

"I see you have knitted another beautiful rug spread on the bush over there, Miss Spider." Mr. Dragonfly said looking at the beautiful spider's web.

"Do you like it?" Miss Spider asked, turning her head to look proudly at her beautiful work.

"It is a lovely rug, Miss Spider. You must have spent many

hours making it. I think you will make a good catch today."

Mr. Dragonfly said.

"I made it wide and fine this time. I sometimes go hungry when my nets are torn by passing animals as they pass by grazing or going for a drink. This time I spread the net away from the animals' way." Miss Spider told her friends.

"Well, this one seems out of the way of many animals. I think this time you will catch a good lunch." Miss Wasp said.

 "Well, I think I should be on my way now." Mrs. Ladybird said.

"Oh, we should all be going to our daily work indeed" Mr. Dragonfly flapped his wings to leave.

 "Good bye Bee." The insects said their goodbyes.

"Good bye Beetle." Mrs. Ladybird called.

"Not so fast, wait a little!" A shaky voice called.

"Oh, look who is coming! Her Royal Highness Mrs. Preying mantis!" exclaimed Mr. Beetle.

"We were about to leave, late comer!" Miss Wasp teased ready to fly away.

"Good morning, everyone! Isn't it good to see you all?" Mrs. Preying Mantis said cheerfully walking carefully towards the other insects.

"It is a lovely morning! I heard voices and thought I should

catch up with the latest news, so I hurried over." Mrs.

Preying Mantis said.

"Well, we were just talking about the usual housework and family." Miss Spider explained.

"It is good to meet often and have a little chat and laughter," Mrs. Ladybird said.

"Yes, it is nice to meet with friends. It can be quite lonely here in the valley," nodded Mrs. Preying Mantis.

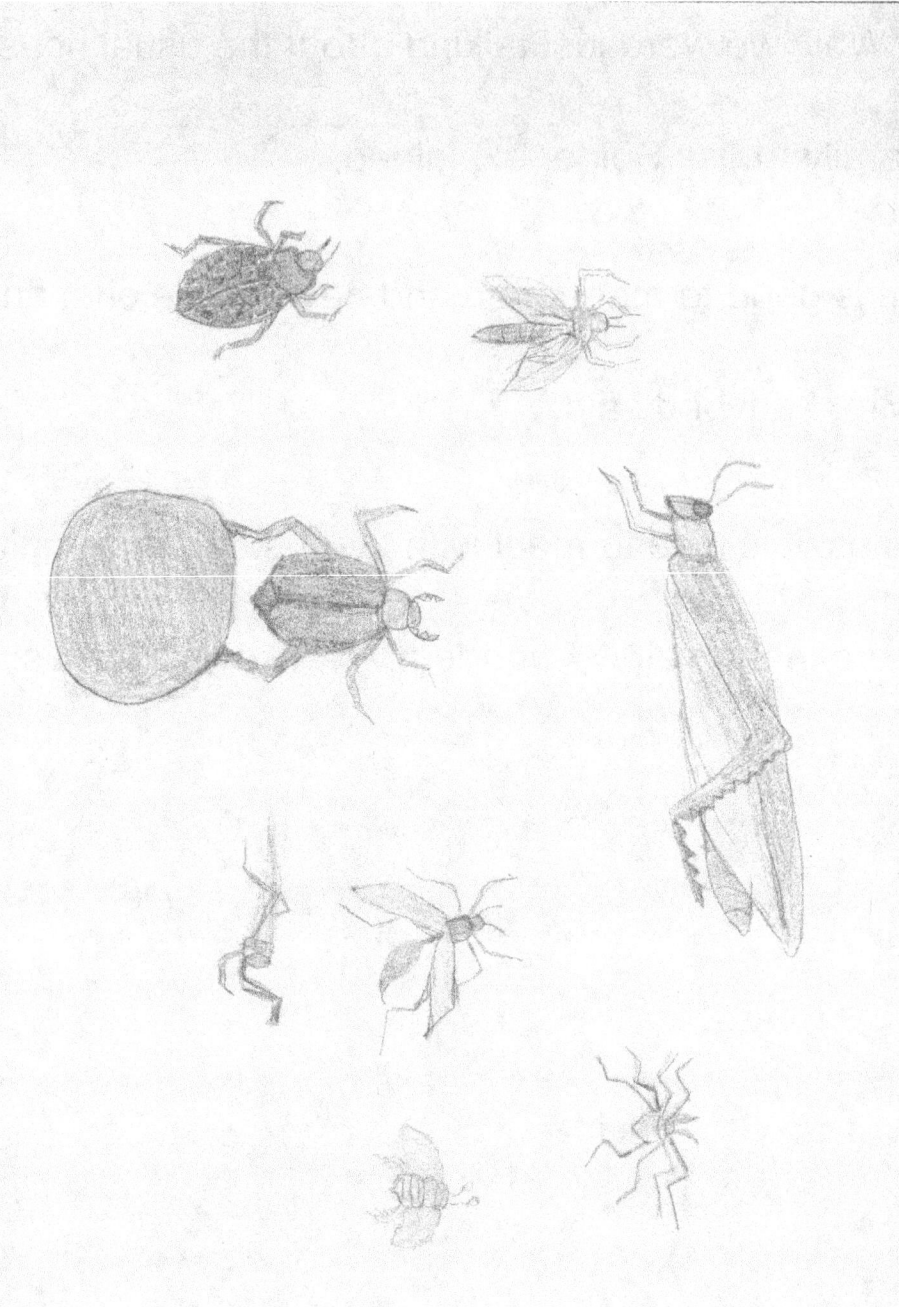

"Tomorrow can we meet by the red flowers near the large rock before the pond?" asked Mr. Dragonfly. "That is a good place to meet. We can then have a drink before we go back to our everyday work." They all agreed.

"Be careful of lizards basking in the sun on the rock," warned Mr. Dragonfly.

"Miss Wasp, can you fly over the rock twice before we gather and tell us if it is safe to get to the flowers?" asked Mrs. Ladybird.

"That is a good idea. I can also come early and look out for enemies before we meet." Mr. Busy Bee said.

'I have an idea.' Mrs. Preying Mantis raised her arm. I think Miss Spider can be a very good security watch. Miss Spider my dear, you could do your crotchet work around the pool while looking out for enemies. You can warn us if there is danger, won't you?

The friends agreed.

They said their goodbyes and went on their separate ways.